George Frideric
HANDEL

LET THY HAND BE STRINGTHENED

Coronation Anthem II

HWV 259

Arranged by

Friedrich Chrysander

Edited by

Clark McAlister

Vocal Score
Klavierauszug

SERENISSIMA MUSIC, INC.

PREFACE

This edition of Handel's *Coronation Anthems* is based upon that of Friedrich Chrysander for the first Handel-Gesellschaft. We have accepted his basic text of these works, choosing only to revise and clarify it in the following aspects:

1. Suggestions for optional overdotting, according to our general understanding of baroque performance practice. These overdottings are shown above the first staff of each score system, and should be applied to those voices and/or instruments within that system as appropriate. These optional overdottings, when appropriate, are shown in the parts and in the vocal score which accompanies this revised edition in the same manner.

2. Tacit correction of a few errors of pitch and obvious inconsistencies of rhythm.

3. Clarification of the use of bassoons within the bass-line group of instruments. The bassoon parts which accompany this revised score have been prepared according to the principles set forth by Adam Carse in *The Orchestra in the XVIII Century*.

4. Preparation of a keyboard realization of Handel's figured bass. The original version of this edition of these anthems included only a keyboard reduction of the orchestral texture prepared by Im. Faisst, which of course is not what is required for stylistic performance of this music. The performance material for this revised edition includes a realization for organ of the figured bass.

Clark McAlister
August, 1986

VERSES

1. Let thy hand be strengthened 1

2. Let justice and judgement 9

3. Allelujah! 15

Duration: ca.6 minutes

Composed August-September 1727

First performance: October 22, 1727

London, Westminster Abbey

Coronation of King George II

Chapel Royal Soli, Chorus, Orchestra, Composer (conductor)

ISBN: 978-1-60874-203-5

©Copyright 1986 Clark McAlister.

Previously issued by E.F. Kalmus as A2637.

LET THY HAND BE STRENGTHENED

HWV 259

George Frideric Handel
Arranged by Friedrich Chrysander
Edited by Clark McAlister

SERENISSIMA MUSIC, INC.

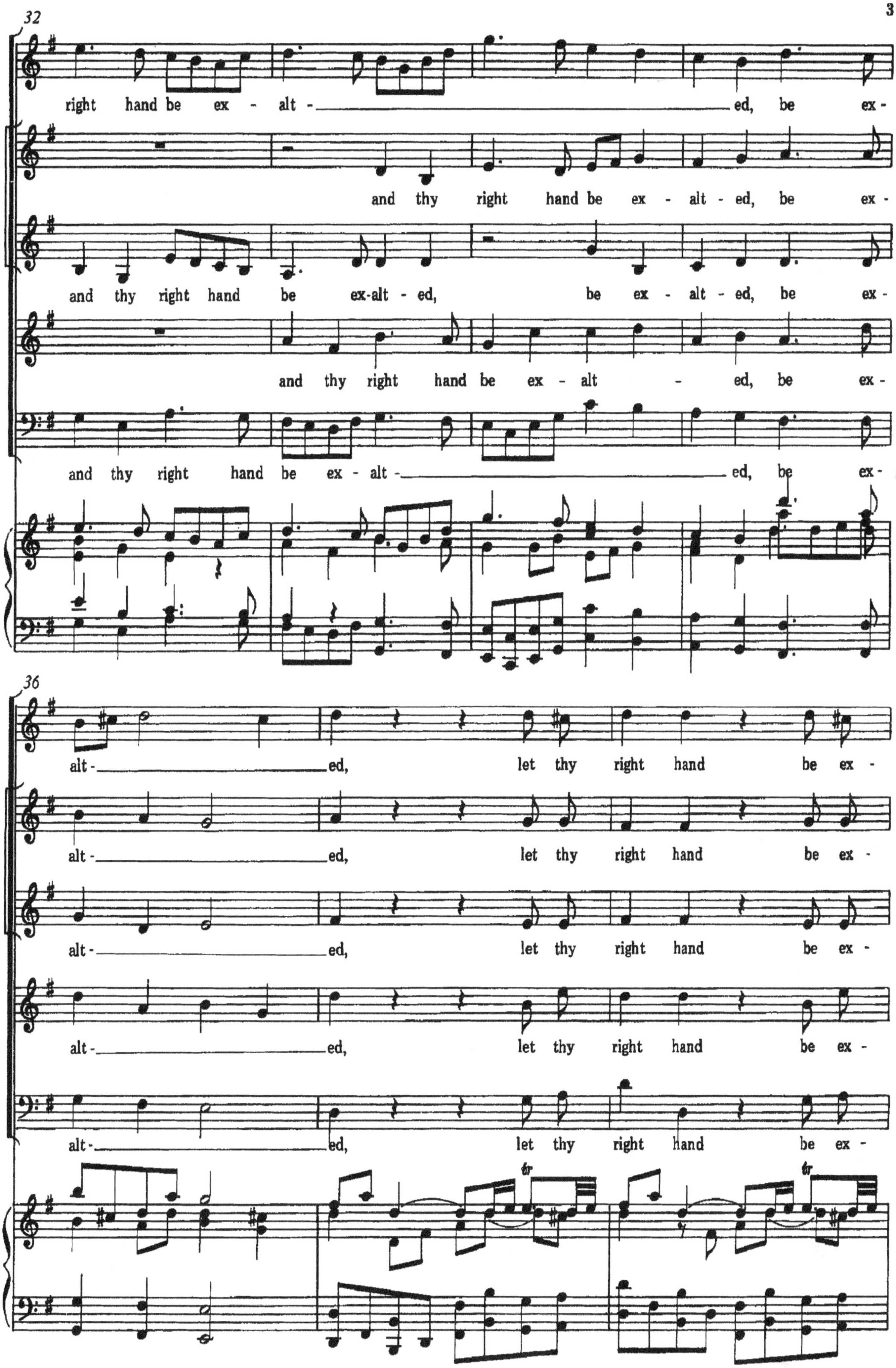
32
right hand be ex - alt - ed, be ex -
and thy right hand be ex - alt - ed, be ex -
and thy right hand be ex-alt - ed, be ex - alt - ed, be ex -
and thy right hand be ex - alt - ed, be ex -
and thy right hand be ex - alt - ed, be ex -
36
alt - ed, let thy right hand be ex -
alt - ed, let thy right hand be ex -
alt - ed, let thy right hand be ex -
alt - ed, let thy right hand be ex -
alt - ed, let thy right hand be ex -
tr
tr

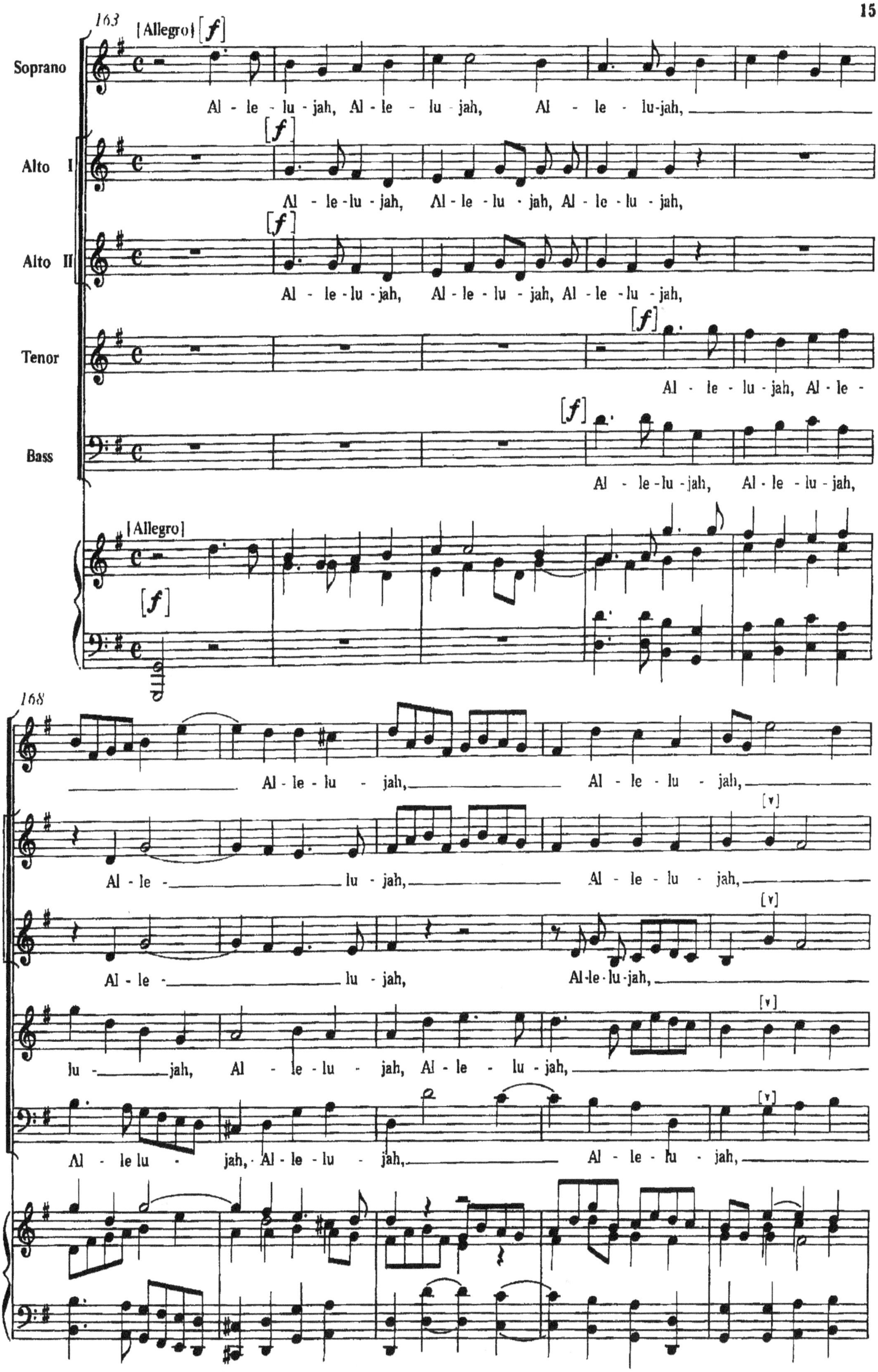
163
[Allegro] [f]
Soprano
Al - le - lu - jah, Al - le - lu - jah, Al - le - lu-jah,
Alto I
[f]
Al - le-lu - jah, Al - le - lu - jah, Al - le - lu - jah,
Alto II
[f]
Al - le-lu - jah, Al - le - lu - jah, Al - le - lu - jah,
Tenor
[f]
Al - le - lu - jah, Al - le -
Bass
[f]
Al - le-lu - jah, Al - le - lu - jah,
[Allegro]
[f]
168
Al - le - lu - jah, Al - le - lu - jah,
Al - le - lu - jah, Al - le - lu - jah,
Al - le - lu - jah, Al-le-lu-jah,
lu - jah, Al - le - lu - jah, Al - le - lu - jah,
Al - le lu - jah, Al - le - lu - jah, Al - le - lu - jah,

www.ingramcontent.com/pod-product-compliance
Lightning Source LLC
Chambersburg PA
CBHW081600040426
42444CB00012B/3174